# EARTHQUAKES

## DANIEL ROGERS

RAINTREE
STECK-VAUGHN
PUBLISHERS
A Steck-Vaughn Company

Austin, Texas

Published by Raintree Steck-Vaughn Publishers,
an imprint of Steck-Vaughn Company

Library of Congress Cataloging-in-Publication Data
Rogers, Daniel.
Earthquakes / Daniel Rogers.
     p.    cm.—(Geography starts here)
     Includes bibliographical references and index.
     Summary: Explains what causes earthquakes, how they are
     measured and predicted, and the effects they can have on
     people and the environment.
     ISBN 0-8172-5546-X
     1. Earthquakes—Juvenile literature.
     [1. Earthquakes.]
     I. Title. II. Series.
     QE521.3.R64 1999
     551.22—dc21               98-28895

Printed in Italy. Bound in the United States.
1 2 3 4 5 6 7 8 9 0 03 02 01 00 99

Picture Acknowledgments
Page 1: Rex/Novedades/Sipa. 4: Rex/Rasmussen/Sipa. 5: FLPA/Steve McCutcheon. 7: Rex. 8: Rex/Butler/Baue. 9: Vinay
Parelkas/Dinodia/OSF. 11: Photri. 12: Rex/Vladimir Sichov/Sipa. 13: Getty Images/Paul Chesley. 14: FLPA/Steve
McCutcheon. 16: Associated Press/Katsumi Kasahara. 17: Topham/AP. 18: Warren Faidley/OSF. 19: Getty
Images/Leverett Bradley. 20: Rex/Today. 21, 22: Rex/Sipa. 23: Rex/Gropp/Sipa. 25: Photri. 27: Science Photo
Library/David Parker. 28: Photri/NASA. 29: Science Photo Library/David Parker. Cover: Rex/Iwasa/Sipa. Illustrations:
Peter Bull and Tony Townsend.

The title page photo shows people being rescued after an earthquake in Mexico City in 1985.

# CONTENTS

# EARTH-SHATTERING

When an earthquake happens, the ground may start to rumble and shake. The shaking often lasts for only a few seconds, but it can cause terrible damage.

Each year there are more than a million earthquakes. Most of them are too small to notice. Others cause a little damage. Only a few earthquakes are big enough to bring death and great destruction.

People rescue their belongings from their shattered homes after an earthquake in San Francisco, in 1989.

ALL OK HERE

An earthquake has
cracked apart this road
in Alaska.

# THE WORLD'S EARTHQUAKES

The earth's surface layer, or crust, is made up of pieces called plates. Although they are made of solid rock, the plates are not fixed in one place—they are moving all the time.

The plates move because they are floating on hot, melted rocks in a layer called the mantle, beneath the earth's crust.

Most earthquakes happen where two of the earth's plates meet. In 1998 two strong earthquakes hit Afghanistan, causing terrible damage.

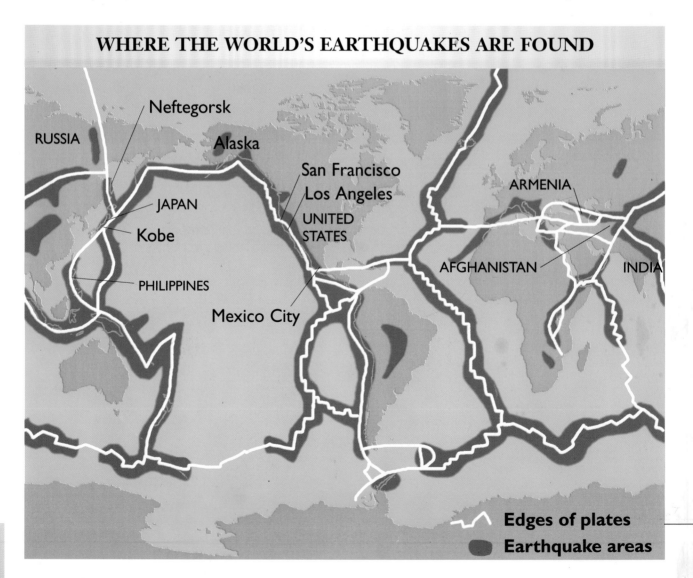

## WHERE THE WORLD'S EARTHQUAKES ARE FOUND

Neftegorsk

RUSSIA

Alaska

San Francisco
Los Angeles

ARMENIA

JAPAN

UNITED
STATES

Kobe

AFGHANISTAN

INDIA

PHILIPPINES

Mexico City

∧∨ **Edges of plates**

● **Earthquake areas**

This railroad bridge in Kobe, Japan, was destroyed by an earthquake in 1995.

Being in a strong earthquake is terrifying. First, there is a loud, deep rumbling sound. Then, the ground begins to shake and crack open. Sometimes it moves up and down in waves, like ripples on a pond.

Buildings, bridges, and some roads rock and shake until they collapse. People have to run for their lives.

This road crashed down on top of another during the 1994 earthquake in Los Angeles.

These buildings were turned to rubble by an earthquake in Maharashtra, India, in 1993.

# What Causes an Earthquake?

Where the earth's plates push together, the rocks do not always slide past each other smoothly. Sometimes they get stuck. The forces pushing them build up until something has to give.

A diagram showing how the rocks move along a fault in an earthquake

Buildings damaged

Power cables broken

Ground cracks open

Layers of rock

Fault

Shock waves spread out from the focus of the earthquake

Strong forces break rocks apart

Focus (center) of the earthquake

## FEEL THE FORCE

Put the palm of your hand on a smooth tabletop and press down. As you push down, try to slide your hand forward along the table. Does it slide smoothly or jerk suddenly and then stop again? Imagine your hand and the table are rocks pushing against each other. Do you see now how an earthquake starts?

A man in California measuring how far the road has moved in an earthquake

Suddenly, the rocks break apart with a huge jolt that sets off an earthquake. Earthquakes usually happen deep underground, but they send out strong shock waves in all directions. Some of these shock waves reach the surface and make the ground shake.

# The Power of Earthquakes

Some earthquakes are much stronger than others. The strength of an earthquake is measured using the Richter scale. An earthquake measuring 2 or less on the Richter scale is too weak to feel. Earthquakes of 7 or more are extremely powerful and can cause great damage.

The earthquake that struck Kobe, Japan, in 1995 measured 7.2 on the Richter scale.

A man testing a concrete wall to see how badly it would be damaged if an earthquake struck

Another way of measuring earthquakes is the Mercalli scale. This scale measures how much an earthquake shakes objects and the damage it causes to buildings.

These houses in Anchorage, Alaska, were destroyed by a landslide following a very strong earthquake.

# After an Earthquake

In mountain areas, earthquakes can set off avalanches, landslides, and mudslides, as huge amounts of snow, rock, or mud are loosened by the shaking. They slide down the sides of the mountains, flattening everything in their way.

After a big earthquake, there may be smaller earthquakes, called aftershocks. Sometimes they knock down weakened buildings.

Landslides, mudslides, and avalanches can rush downhill very fast. They destroy buildings and crops in their path.

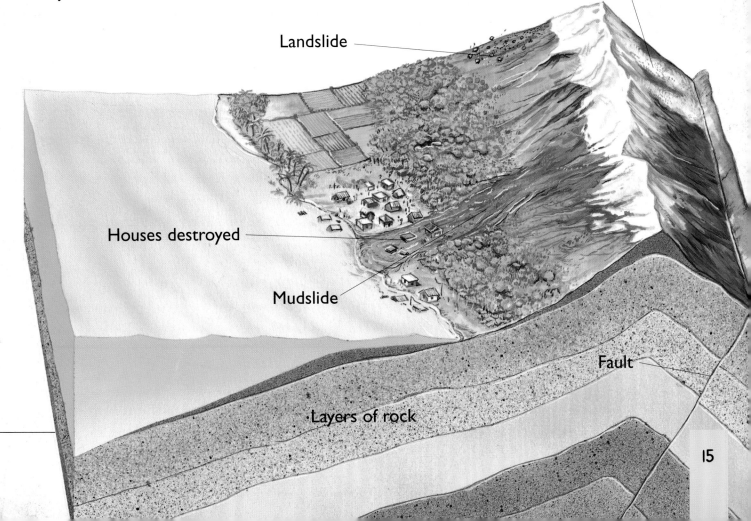

Avalanche

Landslide

Houses destroyed

Mudslide

Fault

Layers of rock

# Tsunamis

Earthquakes under the ocean or near the coast can cause huge waves, called tsunamis. These waves can sweep across the ocean at up to 500 mph (800 km/h).

The harbor on Okushiri Island, Japan, was destroyed by a tsunami in 1993.

A man tries to save some of his possessions after a tsunami flattened his house in the Philippines.

In the open ocean, a tsunami may be only 3 ft. (1 m) high. But by the time it reaches land, it can grow to more than 100 ft. (30 m). When this huge wall of water rushes ashore, it can cause terrible damage.

# PEOPLE AND EARTHQUAKES

A powerful earthquake can have a terrible effect on people's lives. Their houses, schools, hospitals, factories, and offices may be flattened. Roads and bridges may be too damaged to use.

Water pipes, power lines, and gas pipes may be broken. Fires can sweep through a shattered city. They may burn the buildings that were left standing after the earthquake.

An earthquake in California has knocked down power cables and started fires.

This apartment building in Los Angeles was so badly damaged by an earthquake that it had to be torn down.

# Killer Quakes

In an area where there are villages, towns, and cities, a big earthquake can kill thousands of people. Many victims are crushed or buried when buildings collapse.

These people survived an earthquake in Armenia in 1988.

In 1985, a huge earthquake in Mexico City killed more than 7,000 people.

Avalanches and mudslides can destroy whole cities, killing many of the people who live there. Tsunamis flood the land. Many people may drown, and crops are ruined.

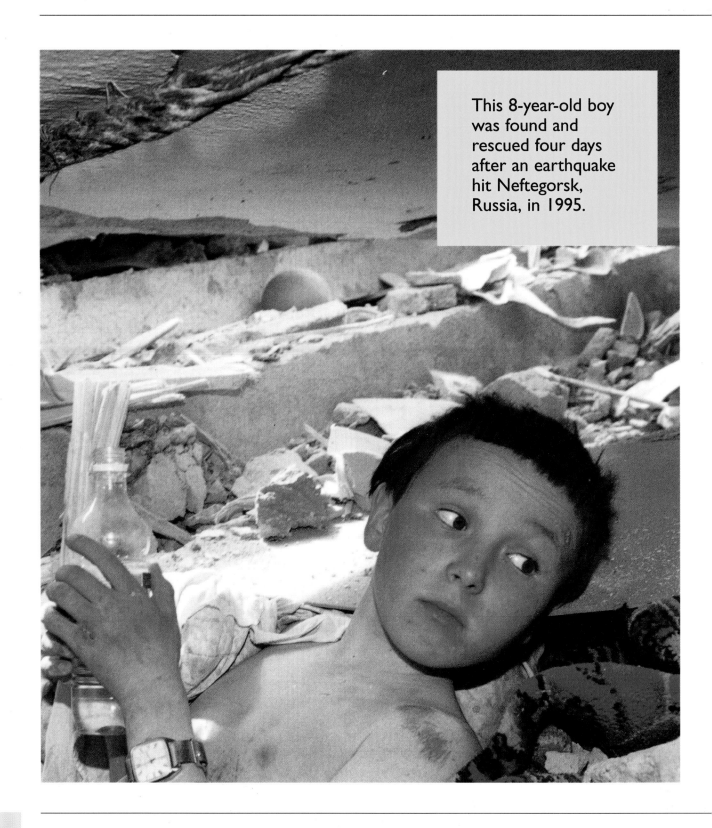

This 8-year-old boy was found and rescued four days after an earthquake hit Neftegorsk, Russia, in 1995.

# Earthquake Rescue

After a major earthquake, help is urgently needed. People who are trapped under collapsed buildings must be found and rescued quickly. Injured people need to be treated.

Food, clean water, blankets, and shelter have to be brought in. Then, power and water supplies must be repaired.

People whose houses were destroyed by an earthquake. Rescue workers have given them tents and blankets.

# Lives on the Line

In 1906 a huge earthquake and fire destroyed San Francisco, killing more than 500 people. In 1989, another earthquake struck. More than 27,000 houses were destroyed, and 62 people died.

Millions of people still live in San Francisco, even though they know there will be more earthquakes in the future.

**GET THE SHAKES**

Imagine you live in an earthquake zone. Get together with your friends and act out what you would do if an earthquake struck.

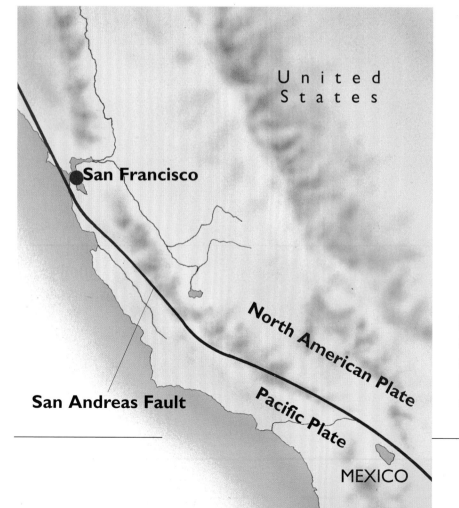

San Francisco suffers earthquakes because the city is on the San Andreas Fault, where two of the earth's plates meet.

People in Mexico were able to read about the earthquake that hit their city just 30 minutes after it happened.

Some places, such as Japan, suffer many earthquakes. Each time earthquakes strike, people rebuild their damaged houses and carry on with their lives.

# CUTTING THE RISK

We cannot keep earthquakes from happening. But we can try to keep them from causing so much destruction. One way is to make buildings that do not collapse in an earthquake.

New buildings must be built so that they don't sink or topple over. Buildings must also be able to sway from side to side during an earthquake, without breaking apart.

In some places where there are many earthquakes, new buildings have to be made earthquake-proof.

**Normal building**

Building shakes

Building breaks apart

People injured or killed

Built on a solid base

**Earthquake-proof building**

Building sways gently

No damage to building

People safe

Built on rubber springs

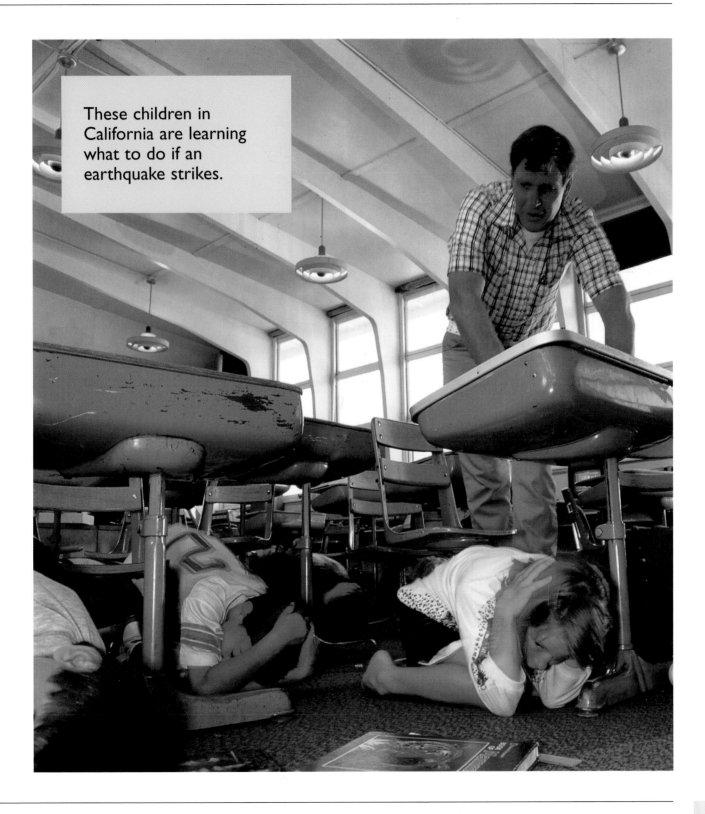

These children in California are learning what to do if an earthquake strikes.

# Predicting Earthquakes

Scientists try to predict earthquakes, using equipment that measures movements in the earth's rocks. But they are not always right. If we knew when earthquakes were about to happen, people could be moved to safety.

Animals may give us warning signs, too. People have noticed that when an earthquake is coming, animals seem to get very restless and even leave the area.

Scientists work on equipment that will help predict earthquakes.

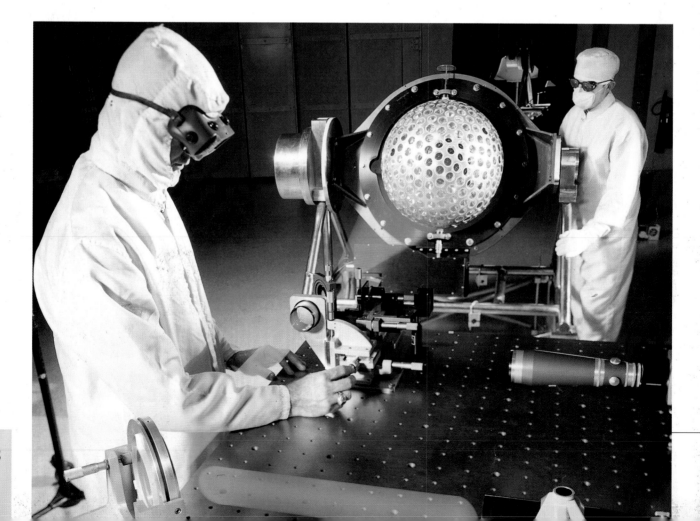

This man is checking equipment that is used to measure movement in the earth's rocks.

# EARTHQUAKE FACTS AND FIGURES

## The deadliest earthquakes
When a massive earthquake struck Shensi Province, China, in 1556, about 830,000 people were killed. The worst earthquake disaster in recent times was also in China. It happened in Tangshan province in 1976. It measured 7.9 on the Richter scale, and about 750,000 people died.

## The greatest destruction
The most damage caused by an earthquake was in the cities of Tokyo and Yokohama, Japan, in 1923. Around 575,000 homes were destroyed by the earthquake, which measured 8.2 on the Richter scale.

## The worst avalanche
When an earthquake struck the mountainous region of Huascarán, Peru, in 1970, it set off a huge avalanche. A 262-ft. (80-m)-high wave of ice, mud, and rock hurtled down the mountains at 250 mph (402 km/h). It struck Yungay, killing over 18,000 people there.

## The worst landslide
In 1920, an earthquake caused a landslide in Kansu Province, China. About 200,000 people were killed.

## The highest tsunami
The tallest tsunami ever caused by an earthquake under the sea was seen off Ishigaki Island, Japan, in 1771. It was estimated to be 279 ft. (85 m) high—about the same as a 25-story building.

## The Richter scale
The Richter scale is used to measure the strength of earthquakes. There is no limit to how high an earthquake can be on it, but the strongest quakes ever, measured 8.6.

## The Mercalli scale
There are 12 levels:
**1** Earthquake not felt.
**2** Felt slightly in upper floors of buildings.
**3** Hanging objects swing.
**4** Strong vibration; cars rock from side to side.
**5** Felt strongly; doors swing.
**6** Books fall from shelves; furniture moves; trees shake.
**7** Difficult to stand; furniture breaks; plaster falls.
**8** Chimneys and walls collapse.
**9** Ground cracks; underground pipes break; many buildings fall.
**10** Most buildings collapse; large landslides.
**11** Railroad lines badly bent; underground pipes wrecked.
**12** Total destruction.

## Further Reading

Christian, Spencer and Felix, Antonia. *Shake, Rattle, and Roll: The World's Most Amazing Volcanoes, Earthquakes, and Other Forces* (Spencer Christian's World of Wonders). New York: John Wiley and Sons, 1997.

Field, Nancy. *Discovering Earthquakes: Mysteries, Secret Codes, Games, Mazes*. Middleton, WI: Dog-Eared Publications, 1995.

Lampton, Christopher. *Earthquake*. Brookfield, CT: Millbrook Press, 1994.

Levy, Matthys. *Earthquake Games: Earthquakes and Volcanoes Explained by Games and Experiments*. New York: Margaret McElderry Books, 1997.

Pope, Joyce. *Earthquakes* (Closer Look At). Brookfield, CT: Millbrook Press, 1998.

Stidworthy, John. *Earthquakes and Volcanoes* (Changing World). San Diego: Thunder Bay Press, 1996.

# GLOSSARY

**Aftershocks** Small earthquakes that happen after the main earthquake.

**Avalanches** Masses of snow and ice that fall down the sides of mountains when they are loosened by a jolt such as an earthquake.

**Crust** The surface layer of the earth.

**Fault** A deep crack in the earth's surface where the rocks have split apart.

**Focus** The place underground where an earthquake starts.

**Landslides** Masses of rocks and soil falling down mountains.

**Mercalli Scale** A way of measuring how much damage an earthquake has caused.

**Mudslides** Masses of mud sliding down the sides of mountains.

**Plates** Large pieces of rock that make up the earth's crust.

**Restless** Worried or unable to remain still.

**Richter Scale** A way of measuring the strength of an earthquake.

**Rubble** Pieces of broken stone, concrete, and bricks from buildings that have fallen down.

**Starvation** Not having enough food to eat.

**Tsunami** An enormous wave caused by a big volcanic explosion or by an underwater earthquake.

A highway near Los Angeles that collapsed in an earthquake. Repairing damaged buildings and roads costs an enormous amount of money.

# INDEX